DEFENSE SECURITY SERVICE

Stakeholder Report 2011

I0410844

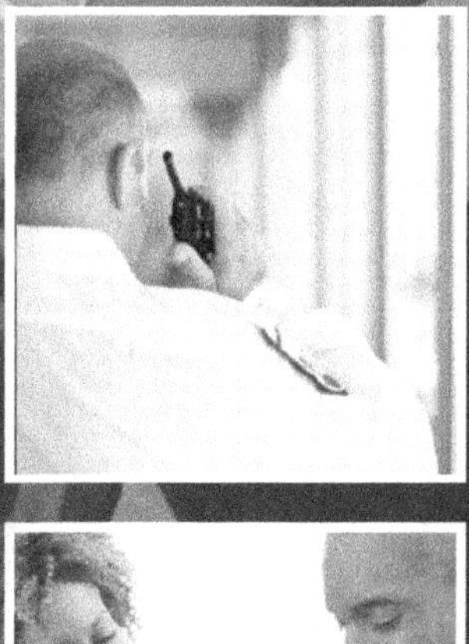

DIRECTOR'S MESSAGE

I am pleased to present our agency's third annual Stakeholder Report, and my first since becoming the DSS Director on Dec. 5, 2010. I am excited about the future of DSS and look forward to joining our stakeholders in forging a stronger partnership.

Since the inaugural issue of the Stakeholder Report, DSS has found this document to be a tremendous tool in sharing successes, priorities and initiatives with employees as well as our Government and Industry Stakeholders. Whether you are new to the agency and industrial security or well acquainted with the history and mission of DSS, I'm sure you will find something of interest in these pages.

For instance, you may have a general understanding of how the Defense Industrial Security Clearance Office (DISCO) processes clearances, but it's also useful to know how incident reports are generated and processed. You'll learn how we stood up a fusion effort within our Counterintelligence Directorate this year and experienced success in "connecting the dots" among our subject matter experts. This report also showcases several counterintelligence case studies and identifies lessons learned that will assist us in taking concrete steps toward improvement and success.

I encourage you to read the report to gain a better understanding of just how much

Stanley L. Sims, DSS Director

DSS has transformed in the past few years. I'm confident you will also gain a better understanding of our goals for the future.

Stanley L. Sims
Director, DSS

DSS Seal

The three divisions of the shield refer to the three basic requirements of all investigations: observation, patient inquiry, and careful examination of the facts.

The eagle, adopted from that used in the seal of DoD, alludes to keenness of vision, strength, and tenacity that symbolizes DSS.

The three arrows, also adopted from the seal of DoD, refer to the Armed Services, comprising the military components of DSS. In crossing over and protectively covering the Pentagon, these arrows represent the DoD wide aspects of the DSS mission.

The color dark blue, the National color, represents the United States, and the color light blue represents DoD, the shade of blue being used by the Defense Department. The pattern indicates the integral unity of the U.S., DoD, and DSS. The color gold (or yellow) is symbolic of zeal and achievement.

On a white disc within a border of blue with gold outer rim is the shield of DSS in full color blazoned above a wreath of laurel and olive proper (as depicted on the DoD seal). Inscribed at top of the white disc is "Defense Security Service" and in the base, in smaller letters, is "United States of America," all letters gold.

The laurel and olives symbolize merit and peace; the color white signifies "deeds worthy of remembrance."

DSS CHARTER

DoD Directive No. 5105.42

The charter for the Defense Security Service, (Department of Defense Directive Number 5105.42), was re-issued and signed by William Lynn, Deputy Secretary of Defense on Aug. 3, 2010. This document serves as the formal statement of the DSS mission and the authorities for DSS activities.

The DSS charter directive states:

> **"** *The DSS, as the DoD Cognizant Security Office for industrial security, shall manage and administer the DoD portion of the National Industrial Security Program (NISP) for the DoD Components and, by mutual agreement, other U.S. Government (USG) departments and agencies; provide security education and training products and services; administer the industrial portion of the DoD Personnel Security Program (PSP), except for those cases that DSS refers to the Defense Office of Hearings and Appeals (DOHA); provide authorized counterintelligence (CI) services; and manage and operate the associated program-specific information technology (IT) systems. The DSS shall also support DoD efforts to improve security programs and processes.* **"**

The August 2010 charter directive replaces the reissuance of the DSS Charter and was the first in over ten years.

HISTORY

Key dates in the history of the Defense Security Service

1965:

On March 8, 1965, the Defense Industrial Security Clearance Office (DISCO) was established when more than 115 Army, Navy and Air Force clearance activities were merged into one facility.

1980:

On Oct. 1, 1980, the Industrial Security Program, the Key Asset Protection Program, the Arms, Ammunition and Explosives Security Program and the Defense Industrial Security Institute were transferred to DIS from the Defense Logistics Agency.

1976:

In 1976, DIS received Congressional direction to phase out all military personnel and become a totally civilian agency.

1972:

On Jan. 1, 1972, the Defense Investigative Service (DIS) was established. DIS was created in response to President Richard M. Nixon's approval of proposals suggesting the reorganization of the national intelligence community and the creation of an "Office of Defense Investigation" to consolidate Department of Defense (DoD) personnel security investigations (PSI).

1984:

On Jan. 1, 1984, the Defense Industrial Security Institute in Richmond was redesignated as the Defense Security Institute.

1993:

On Jan. 6, 1993, President George H.W. Bush signed Executive Order 12829, establishing the National Industrial Security Program (NISP). This program was intended to replace not only the DISP, but also the industrial security programs of the Central Intelligence Agency, the Department of Energy and the Nuclear Regulatory Commission.

In May 1993, DIS established a counterintelligence (CI) office to foster the integration of CI with the DIS security countermeasure mission.

1995:

On April 1, 1995, the National Industrial Security Program Operating Manual (NISPOM) was promulgated as directed by EO 12829. The NISPOM provides baseline standards for the protection of classified information released or disclosed to contractors in connection with classified contracts under the NISP.

On April 19, 1995, the Alfred P. Murrah Building in Oklahoma City was bombed killing 168 people, including DIS employees Bob Westberry, Larry Cottingham, Peter DeMaster, Jean Johnson and Larry Turner of the Oklahoma City Investigative Field Office. DIS dedicated two living memorials to them – an Oklahoma Red Bud Tree at the DSS Headquarters building and a cherry tree at the Tidal Basin in Washington, D.C.

2003:

On Feb. 4, 2003, the Commission of the Council on Occupational Education (COE), a national accrediting authority recognized by the Department of Education, granted accreditation to the Defense Security Service Academy. The DSS Academy was reaccredited in 2009.

2005:

On Feb. 20, 2005, DoD transferred the personnel security investigations (PSI) functions performed by DSS to the Office of Personnel Management (OPM).

1997:

On Nov. 25, 1997, DIS was redesignated as the Defense Security Service in order to reflect the agency's broader mission and functions, including the industrial security, personnel security, security education, and training missions.

1999:

On July 21, 1999, the Defense Security Service Academy was formally established.

2007:

On Dec. 18, 2007, the Director of DSS was named the functional manager for DoD Security Training.

2009:

On Jan. 15, 2009, the Deputy Secretary of Defense signed a memorandum directing DSS to focus on meeting 21st century industrial security and counterintelligence needs by enhancing and expanding the NISP and reinvigorating the Security Training and Awareness Program.

ORGANIZATIONAL OVERVIEW

Scope of the DSS Mission:

13,333 active, cleared facilities in the National Industrial Security Program (NISP)

Clear and inspect facilities

- 9,448 inspections
- 1,279 new facility clearances granted
- 18,438 accredited systems in industry
- Conduct inspections on behalf of DoD and 23 federal partners

Adjudicate Industry Security Clearances (DISCO)

- 1 million cleared contractor personnel
- 247,444 adjudication actions
- 19.7 days average to process 90% clearances

Fund NISP Personnel Security Investigations

- Estimated $211 million expended in FY10
- Budget for FY11 is $234.1 million

Mitigate Foreign Ownership Control or Influence (FOCI) in Cleared Industry

- 588 FOCI facilities
- 278 FOCI mitigation agreements

Perform Counterintelligence Functions

- 201 known or suspected illicit collectors identified within industry
- 7,002 CI Suspicious Contact Reports
- 660 Intelligence Information Reports

DoD Functional Manager for Security Training

- 127,633 course completions in FY10
- 356,679 course completions FY05-FY10 (1044% increase)
- 149 course completions by sponsored foreign nationals
- Catalog of 68 courses serving DoD and Industry
- 62% increase in course catalog since FY05

Professionalization

- Develop Certification Program for DoD Security Professionals
- Facilitate the DoD Security Training Council

All data is FY10 year-end data.

DSS LOCATIONS

* *DSS Field Offices*

* DSS Resident Offices

Capital Region, Arlington, VA

Linthicum, MD
Crystal City, VA
Chantilly, VA

Northern Region, Boston, MA

Groton, CT
Shelton, CT
Andover, MA
Boston, MA
Detroit, MI
Fort Snelling, MN
Mt. Laurel, NJ
Picatinny Arsenal, NJ
Syracuse, NY

Watervliet-Arsenal, NY
Williamsville, NY
Cincinnati, OH
Cleveland, OH
Dayton, OH
Fort Indiantown Gap, PA
McClure, PA
Philadelphia, PA
Sewickley, PA
Milwaukee, WI

Western Region, San Diego, CA

Anchorage, AK
Phoenix, AZ
Tucson, AZ
Camarillo, CA

Cypress, CA
Encino, CA
Pasadena, CA
San Diego, CA
Sunnyvale, CA
Travis Air Force Base, CA
Colorado Springs, CO
Denver, CO
Honolulu, HI
Albuquerque, NM
Seattle, WA
Bountiful, UT

Southern Region, Irving, TX

Huntsville, AL
Homestead, FL
Hurlburt Field, FL

Jacksonville, FL
Melbourne, FL
Orlando, FL
Tampa, FL
Smyrna, GA
Chicago, IL
Kansas City, KS
St. Louis, MO
Gulfport, MS
Charlotte, NC
Raleigh, NC
Offutt Air Force Base, NE
Oklahoma City, OK
Charleston, SC
San Antonio, TX
Irving, TX
Hampton, VA
Virginia Beach, VA

ACHIEVEMENTS

DSS continually assesses the effectiveness of its oversight of the industrial security program to ensure the most robust mechanisms for the protection of classified information in industry are in place. DSS achieved a number of notable successes during FY10 and is particularly proud of the following

- DSS Counterintelligence referrals resulted in more than **200 investigations** or operations by federal law enforcement and intelligence agencies (**an increase of over 300 percent from FY09**).

- Decreased the average time needed to process a Foreign Ownership Control or Influence (FOCI) case **from 256 days to 120 days**.

- Decreased the FOCI case backlog (cases over 120 days old) **from 93 to 23 cases**.

- Established tailored inspections for FOCI facilities and **completed the first corporate-wide reviews**.

- Continued to implement the Facilities of Interest List (FIL) to prioritize and tailor inspections to ensure the most

sensitive technologies are protected. **DSS completed all FIL I and FIL II category security reviews.**

- **Created a DSS Operations Analysis Group** to identify gaps in information about NISP personnel and industrial security clearances, and maximize collaboration across the agency in filling these gaps.

- **Initiated nationwide beta testing of the Security Fundamentals Professional Certification**, which is the first of four Security Professional Education Development (SPēD) Certifications. The beta testing will provide data needed to finalize the scores and exam for the formal launch of the program.

- Sponsored a DoD Security Manager's Conference attended by more than **500 security professionals** from across the Department of Defense.

- **Completed the programmatic control transition of the information technology systems** supporting personnel security investigations to the Defense Manpower Data Center.

Tailored Inspections

All facilities cleared under the NISP are required to undergo periodic security inspections by DSS. To create a more efficient process and dispel the perception that DSS conducts "checklist" inspections, DSS continues to refine its inspection methodology.

The goal of a security inspection should be an integrated visit from DSS to the right facility at the right time with appropriate resources resulting in a more effective, meaningful inspection.

As a part of the inspection evolution, DSS is now conducting corporate-wide inspections of companies with multiple facilities under Foreign Ownership Control or Influence (FOCI). This approach gives both DSS and the company a big picture view of the security status of its cleared facilities.

Each team consists of an Industrial Security Representative, Information Systems Security Professional, Field Counterintelligence Specialist, and a Senior Action Officer specializing in FOCI. DSS developed a standardized FOCI Inspection Action Plan which detailed pre-inspection research/actions. Completion of the Action Plan ensures that all team members are informed of current FOCI issues at the company.

Information from the inspection is shared with the company senior leadership and security team on a regular basis. The information includes results of the inspection, notable best practices, serious NISP findings and any FOCI issues. The purpose is to provide feedback on the compliance record of the company from the previous quarter.

Feedback from the first round of corporate-wide inspections was extremely positive, and company senior leadership appreciated DSS efforts in developing trends across facilities.

DSS began tailored inspections of FOCI facilities first because there are approximately 588 cleared facilities with FOCI considerations. FOCI oversight is complex and DSS wanted to ensure consistency across FOCI facilities. DSS will develop a similar inspection methodology for freight forwarding companies and trusted foundry and Arms, Ammunition and Explosives (AA&E) facilities.

DSS expands financial analysis capability

The globalization of the economic market has resulted in a spider web of complex financial mechanisms, which can mask foreign ownership, control or influence on cleared companies. To get a clearer picture of a company's status and financial condition, the Assessment and Evaluation (A&E) Division of the Industrial Policy and Programs Directorate (IP) is looking more closely at companies' financial relationships.

The A&E Division is conducting financial assessments on business entities seeking and currently performing work on DoD classified contracts to expand awareness of possible foreign influence. Since DSS has traditionally relied largely on information provided by the company through self-reporting, DSS may not have the most current information needed to make a sound assessment.

In performing the assessments, the A&E Division:

- Reviews company audited financial statements to verify self-reported financial information

- Validates initial and periodic company self-reported financial and ownership information through open source and Government-owned database research;

- Identifies complex financial instruments and relationships that may impact FOCI thresholds, e.g., derivative instruments; hedge funds; managed accounts; sovereign wealth funds; private equity investment; funds-of-funds; and, "off balance sheet transactions"

Much of the information that DSS now analyzes is pulled from Government regulatory agencies and commercially available sources. Additionally, the A&E Division will use classified U.S. Government data integration platforms to identify and evaluate complex financial relationships to clarify or uncover the source of a cleared company's capital.

When looking at the condition of cleared companies, DSS analysts search out key indicators that determine whether a company is financially vulnerable or has undergone a material change without notifying DSS. If a U.S. company is being, or is likely to be, bought by a foreign entity, the A&E analysis allows DSS to assess whether the U.S subsidiary is capable of operating as a viable business entity separate from the foreign owner.

To expand its capabilities, the A&E Division has entered into agreements or formed partnerships with the Defense Contract

Management Agency, to share financial data on business entities seeking and currently performing on DoD classified contracts; and the Office of the Undersecretary of Defense for Acquisition, Technology and Logistics, Industrial Policy Directorate, to share industrial base financial analyses, merger and acquisition assessment and the impact of new investment instruments on determining FOCI.

DSS has also held discussions with the Securities and Exchange Commission's Division of Investment Management, on the impact of new financial regulatory laws for hedge funds and private equity firms. And, DSS is working with the U.S. Treasury Department on information sharing arrangements, as well as with the Recovery Accountability & Transparency Board (RATB), to routinely integrate consideration of that organization's database information into the FOCI and facility clearance process.

66 *We are now in a new and more complex era, but the partnership with industry is just as critical to our security today. It must be nurtured and encouraged. We need direct dealings and honest dialogue between industry leaders and those of us in the Department.* 99

William J. Lynn III
Deputy Secretary of Defense

New Guide for Field Office Chiefs

DSS Field Office Chiefs (FOCs) must have a fundamental understanding of industrial security and the DSS mission and also manage personnel, resources and schedules. Visits conducted under the Staff Assessment Visit (SAV) program found that each Field Office was being run differently. While the DSS Industrial Security Operating Manual provides detailed internal instructions for DSS personnel on providing NISP oversight and services, no formal guidance existed related to managing a Field Office. Help arrived for FOCs in the form of a Standard Operating Procedure (SOP) for FOCs. The first version was issued in September 2009 and established the fundamental principles and practices for all FOCs to follow. It also established uniform management standards for DSS Industrial Security personnel.

The goal of the SOP is to state management principles and procedures by drawing on the best practices established by offices that have demonstrated consistent success. The SOP is not intended to be a "management by the numbers" guide. The initial SOP was updated in April 2010 and will continue to be revised as industrial security policies and regulations affecting office management change.

On a practical level, the SOP includes a

wide range of topics including employee performance appraisals, managing workflow, documenting overtime, maintaining a correct badge, and credential inventory. However, the majority of the document is devoted to setting internal standards and procedures to manage oversight of the National Industrial Security Program.

DSS launches SF-328 review

In 2008, DSS stood up the Foreign Ownership, Control or Influence (FOCI) Analytic Division (FAD) to ensure all available information was analyzed and applied prior to determining the proper risk mitigation strategy for companies with FOCI. Central to this effort is the analysis of the Certificate Pertaining to Foreign Interests (SF-328) submitted by all companies upon entry into the National Industrial Security Program (NISP).

Normally, DSS Field Offices collect the SF-328s and supporting documentation and only those packets that have identified or suspected of undisclosed FOCI are forwarded to the Headquarters FOCI Operations Division. In May 2010, the FAD, in conjunction with the DSS Field Operations Directorate, initiated a beta test with four field offices in which all SF-328 packets, regardless of the responses, were forwarded to the FAD for analysis.

By reviewing all of the SF-328s with the additional analytical resources at its disposal, the FAD identified discrepancies between actual and reported FOCI information in approximately 29 percent of the cases examined. While not all of the discrepancies were serious and not all of these cases ultimately required mitigation, the results were sufficient to justify changing procedures so that all SF-328s will be sent to

the FAD for analysis in the future. This action reduces the workload of Industrial Security Representatives (ISRs) and Regional Senior Action Officers and will serve to validate the company-supplied information relied upon by DSS in making industrial security oversight decisions.

Once the new process is fully implemented, ISRs will continue to be the principal players in the process, and this process should not create additional requirements for field personnel. Upon completion of the FAD's review, the ISR is notified of the results of the review. If no unreported or reported FOCI requiring mitigation is found, the process of granting an FCL will continue as usual and the facility will be cleared if it meets all other facility clearance requirements. When the FAD finds FOCI requiring mitigation, the normal headquarters mitigation process starts. In cases where cross-directorate issues are found, the case will be forwarded to the DSS Operations Analysis Group for action.

The beta test results indicate enhanced scrutiny of SF-328s will further ensure FOCI is identified and will likely result in more mitigation actions. With full implementation, the FAD is actively identifying and monitoring FOCI, which will help ensure that FOCI is identified and properly mitigated.

Incident Reports

Paragraph 1-302 a., National Industrial Security Program Operating Manual (NISPOM), February 28, 2006, states: "Adverse Information. Contractors shall report adverse information coming to their attention concerning any of their cleared employees."

This NISPOM paragraph sets forth the requirement that cleared facilities report adverse information concerning their cleared employees — including persons nominated by the facilities for clearances — to DSS, specifically to the Defense Industrial Security Clearance Office (DISCO). The requirement is simply stated, but the action taken behind the scenes by the DISCO adjudicators is a precise, complex process that can result in the suspension of a cleared contractor's eligibility for access to classified information. Once a person has been submitted for a clearance or eligibility has been granted, DISCO depends on the cleared contractor facility to provide information that may impact on the status of an employee's clearance.

Adverse information, also known as an "incident report," should be submitted by the company's Facility Security Officer via the Joint Personnel Adjudication System (JPAS). However, government agencies can also report the information via JPAS, and persons, including co-workers or other sources may, and do, provide adverse information to DISCO directly via email, postal mail or telephonically.

Once entered into JPAS, the incident report flags an individual's JPAS record. Typical incident reports cover such things as driving under the influence, formal criminal charges or financial problems. They can be very specific and detailed or very vague. In the latter case, it is incumbent upon the adjudicator to flush out the details and decide on a course of action.

When a DISCO adjudicator receives the incident report, he/she typically takes one of three actions:

1. **Favorably adjudicates the issue.** For example, when an individual's wages are garnished for child support in a state that requires an automatic garnishment and there are no other indicators of financial problems, the red flag is removed from the individual's record and no further action is taken.

2. **Requests that the investigative service provider (usually OPM) open an investigation into the incident.** For instance, in a case where an individual was recently arrested, the DISCO adjudicator will

normally take no further action until the law enforcement investigation is completed and a final review is conducted of the facts surrounding the reported incident. In this case, the individual still retains his eligibility, but his JPAS record has a red flag reflecting the pending nature of an incident report.

3. Suspends the clearance eligibility and requests an investigation. This interim suspension is taken by the DSS Director in very serious incidents, such as when an individual is convicted of a serious crime or has shown a clear disregard for procedures governing the handling of classified information. The case could still ultimately be favorably adjudicated, but until that time, all access to classified information must be suspended by the Facility Security Officer.

DISCO receives about 8,000 incident reports a year and typically recommends about 120 interim suspensions a year to the DSS Director.

All actions, to include incident reports that were favorably adjudicated, are tracked in JPAS. This paper trail assists an adjudicator in identifying the development of trends or anomalies. For instance, an individual may have had incidents reported at multiple companies, but unless an adjudicator can see each incident, connections cannot be found. A minor incident at one company may not be of concern, but when similar incidents occur at three separate companies, they begin to form a pattern of suspicious or inappropriate behavior.

The Adjudicative Process

Personnel security adjudicators adhere to the whole-person concept and the Adjudicative Guidelines when making personnel clearance eligibility decisions. Adjudicators receive specialized training on how to interpret and apply the Adjudicative Guidelines for Determining Eligibility for Access to Classified Information. When weighing a decision, DISCO adjudicators have a number of resources at their disposal. For instance, they are required to query the Defense Central Index of Investigations (DCII) for other investigations. They also routinely coordinate with other investigative and adjudicative agencies. The process may take up to six months or more because adjudicators can only make decisions after they receive all appropriate and relevant information.

The job of an adjudicator is very detail-oriented and can involve sifting through voluminous data. DISCO finds derogatory information at various levels of seriousness in approximately 90 percent of the cases it reviews.

"The adjudicative process is the careful weighing of a number of variables known as the whole person concept. Available, reliable information about the person, past and present, favorable and unfavorable, should be considered in reaching a determination. In evaluating the relevance of an individual's conduct, the adjudicator should consider the following factors:

1. The nature, extent, and seriousness of the conduct.

2. The circumstances surrounding the conduct, to include knowledgeable participation.

3. The frequency and recency of the conduct.

4. The individual's age and maturity at the time of the conduct.

5. The voluntariness of participation.

6. The presence or absence of rehabilitation and other pertinent behavioral changes.

7. The motivation for the conduct.

8. The potential for pressure, coercion, exploitation, or duress.

9. The likelihood of continuation of recurrence."

Adjudicative Guidelines:

A: Allegiance to the United States.

B: Foreign influence.

C: Foreign preference.

D: Sexual behavior.

E: Personal conduct.

F: Financial considerations.

G: Alcohol consumption.

H: Drug involvement.

I: Psychological conditions.

J: Criminal conduct.

K: Handling protected information

L: Outside activities.

M: Use of information technology systems.

Staff Assessment Visits bring consistency to Field Offices

During a three-month period in 2010, teams from the Industrial Security Field Operations (ISFO) Quality Assurance Program visited field offices in each region to conduct staff assessment visits (SAV). The SAV process involved conducting internal interviews, facility folder reviews, and research in the Industrial Security Facilities Database followed by discussions with cleared contractor representatives. The intent of the SAVs is to achieve inspection consistency across DSS.

During the visits, the ISFO team implemented a standardized assessment process and trained DSS regional employees to guarantee consistent assessments across the country. These initial assessments were conducted by teams of five to eight people from regions other than that of the office being assessed.

During the visits, the team members conducted one-on-one mentoring and training in the

SAV process so that each region would have the knowledge to conduct visits in the future.

SAV results are furnished to the ISFO Quality Assurance Office for a DSS-wide analysis with the intent of identifying best practices and areas that might require process improvements or guidance revision, and to measure and evaluate the effectiveness of the regional inspection process.

New Industrial Security courses better train IS Representatives for the field

The DSS Industrial Security Mentoring Program and Industrial Security Specialist Course (ISSC) were initially established in 2001. The mentoring program was designed to ensure new IS Reps could quickly gain knowledge about their roles and responsibilities through a structured program of on the job training and workbook exercises that would prepare them to attend the instructor-led ISSC held at the DSS Academy.

As DSS transforms to meet the security challenges of today and the future, training must also change. As part of this transformation and as new employees are brought on board, IS Reps and Information System Security Personnel (ISSP) are expected to be more productive sooner and develop knowledge and capabilities more quickly.

With those goals in mind, the DSS Academy (DSSA) developed the Fundamentals of Industrial Security Levels 1 and 2 (FISL-1 and FISL-2). FISL-1 replaces the mentoring program, while FISL-2 is designed to replace the ISSC.

FISL-1 is significantly more structured and challenging than the mentoring program and provides an increased level of accountability for students, their supervisors, and the DSS

Academy staff. It is a blended learning experience that incorporates independent actions (reading, web-based training courses, writing assignments, quizzes, and exams) with team actions (ride-alongs and observed participation). It also involves the Field Office Chief, a lead advisor, other members of the Field Office, and a DSS Academy instructor. Nearly 50 students are currently enrolled in FISL-1, and they complete the course in approximately five to six months.

Upon completion of FISL-1, students should be able to conduct non-complex survey actions and conduct inspections of non-complex, non-possessing facilities independently. These new IS Reps and ISSPs should be productive before they attend the instructor-facilitated (FISL-2) course at the Academy. The curriculum of FISL-2 builds upon the performance, knowledge, and skills learned and employed in FISL-1. Sixty-three students have completed FISL-2 to date.

Center for the Development of Security Excellence (CDSE)

In March 2010, the Director of the Defense Security Service (DSS) formally established the Center for Development of Security Excellence (CDSE). The CDSE will conduct security education, training and professional development functions and be responsible for administering the DoD Security Professional Education Development Program (SPēD), the DoD Personnel Security Adjudicator Certification Program, and for carrying out security training program assessments and development functions.

DoD Instruction 3305.13, "DoD Security Training," assigns the Director, DSS, as the functional manager responsible for the execution and maintenance of DoD security training. The DSS Future Options Study expanded on the 2007 DoD Instruction and specifically suggested the development of a "Security Community Center of Excellence." On January 15, 2009, the Deputy Secretary of Defense directed DSS to carry out the recommendations of the Future Options Study to include "reinvigorating the Security Education Training and Awareness Program."

The CDSE will assume the training previously provided by the Academy in addition to its other missions and functions serving the security education, training, and professionalization requirements of the DoD and cleared industry. The DSS Academy's focus will shift to the training and education of the internal DSS industrial security workforce.

In addition, while the CDSE will continue the missions and functions of the Defense Security Service's security education, training and awareness missions, the Center will also add the following:

- Professional development throughout the career of DoD security personnel

- Certification of security professionals through the Security Professional Education Development (SPēD) Program and the DoD Personnel Security Adjudication Program

- Graduate-level courses and higher education opportunities aimed to develop leaders of the DoD security community

- Repository for DoD security resources

- Forum for enhanced communication within the DoD security community

- Consulting support for the DoD community

The CDSE reaches customers through a variety of methods, including classroom and web-based training and forums including conferences and events, mailing lists, and the internet.

Training Down Under

The Center for Development of Security Excellence (CDSE) delivered the Introduction to Special Access Programs (SAPs) Course to 14 Australian citizens in August in Canberra, Australia. This was the culmination of a long coordination process that started in February 2010 with the endorsement of the U.S./Australian Defense Counsel in response to a request from the Australian Department of Defence for the United States to provide training assistance. This international effort was the first of its kind for the CDSE.

The training was provided to Australian personnel in support of the Joint Strike Fighter (JSF) Program. The goals were to provide more cost effective training and establish the staff needed to honor approved security commitments for joint U.S./Australian programs.

Although the course was conducted at the unclassified level, Australia provided a SAP-accredited environment to conduct the training, which highlighted to students the importance of such training. It also allowed students to gain first-hand knowledge of the experience of being employed in a SAP facility.

The Australian Program Manager met with CDSE personnel following course completion and recognized the course as "a good model for the future" that resulted in significant savings for the Australian government because it involved the right people at the right time.

The Australian Program Manager anticipates requesting training for an additional 15 people in FY11. Other courses may also be requested to include parts of the SAP curriculum, the Security Awareness for Educators (SAFE) course, and a risk management course.

Security Professional Education Development Program

> **❝** *Create a defense intelligence workforce training program that provides the skills and flexibility to leverage all intelligence and security capabilities against the full range of mission requirements.* **❞**

Priority III.1.C under Strategic Goal III
Defense Intelligence Strategy, 2008

In the 2008 Defense Intelligence Strategy, the Under Secretary of Defense for Intelligence (USD(I)) noted the relationship between the skills of the defense and national intelligence workforce and the quality of intelligence products. The Strategy set goals to "… acquire, retain, develop, train, educate, equip, and employ the total workforce effectively and efficiently in support of defense and national intelligence requirements."

To accomplish these goals, the DoD Security Training Council (DSTC), chaired by DSS, launched the Security Professional Education Development Program (SPēD). The SPēD Program is intended to ensure a common set of competencies among security practitioners and to promote interoperability, facilitate professional development and training, and develop a workforce of certified security professionals.

The individual components across the Department are responsible for designating which positions will require the SPēD Certification. When fully deployed, SPēD will provide a clear path to success for security professionals. It will outline training options, job aids, tools, certifications, and certificates based on the career decisions of the security workforce. The SPēD Certification Program is based on functions performed; it is not based on occupational titles or pay grades.

DSS and the DSTC relied on subject matter experts in the various security disciplines (physical, personnel, industrial and information) to design the program. They collectively answered several questions: What skills should be defined? How should the program be structured? What knowledge should practitioners have at various stages of their careers?

The program has four certifications of increasing scope and complexity:

- Security Fundamentals Professional Certification (SFPC)

- Security Asset Protection Professional Certification (SAPPC)

- Security Program Integration Professional Certification (SPIPC)

- Security Enterprise Professional Certification (SEPC)

From September to December 2010, over 900 security practitioners participated in a Beta Test of the Security Fundamentals Professional Certification. DSS will use the results to set baseline test standards, finalize the test structure, and ensure that it meets outside accreditation standards.

The first certification, SFPC, will be operational in early 2011. DSS personnel are looking at test sites across the country — most likely education centers already established on existing military installations — to administer the test. Participants need to register for the program using DSS's online registration ENROL system. Once established, participant progress will be monitored and followed by DSS personnel. The other three SPēD certifications are in development and the SAPPC is scheduled for beta testing during FY11.

Certification candidates have a wide variety of

> **66** *We must recognize there is no 'normal' anymore. What once was routine is anything but. And what once was unusual is becoming all too routine.* **"**
>
> Adm. Mike Mullen
> **Chairman, Joint Chiefs of Staff**

resources designed to inform and assist them through the certification program, including a certification handbook, online training courses, a certification online resource tool, and a diagnostic examination.

Like most certification programs, the SPēD Certification Program has a certification maintenance requirement. Once certified, participants will have to earn a designated number of professional development units (PDUs) every two years. PDUs can be earned through a variety of professional development activities including taking security training courses, attending security conferences, etc.

The SPēD Certification Program will be phased in over a five-year period across the Department. Ultimately, the program will include specialty certifications such as Special Access Programs, Research Technology Protection, etc.

Management of Legacy Personnel Security IT Systems Transferred

This past year DSS transferred programmatic control of the Joint Personnel Adjudication System (JPAS), Defense Central Index of Investigations (DCII), the Secure Web Fingerprint Transmission (SWFT), and the "improved Investigative Records Repository" (iIRR) to the Defense Manpower Data Center (DMDC). The transfer was directed by the Deputy Secretary of Defense in a January 15, 2009 memorandum. Control and responsibility for iIRR and SWFT transferred in May, JPAS in June, and DCII in July.

To ensure the transfer was transparent to the users of the systems with no interruption in service, DSS and DMDC signed a Memorandum of Agreement in February 2010 and established a six-month transition period for the systems. The transition period was necessary as JPAS is a large, complex system with over 116,000 users. This also applied to the other three systems as they had unique technical items to address for their respective transitions.

DSS still continues to operate the systems, performing ongoing maintenance, and implementing system enhancements as provided by DMDC. DSS also still provides Call Center/Help Desk user inquiry and assistance. These remaining functions will transition to DMDC in CY2011. DMDC personnel have "shadowed" DSS personnel, program managers and contractors for the transitioned functions to gain a detailed understanding of the systems procedures and processes for performing maintenance and upgrading systems components and applications. The original MOA is being amended to incorporate other items during the remaining transition period.

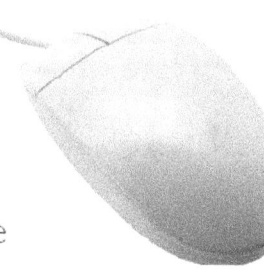

New Direction for Counterintelligence

In FY10, DSS continued to emphasize the agency's work with industry to support national security, secure the nation's technological base, and oversee the protection of classified information in the hands of cleared contractors.

DSS and its Counterintelligence (CI) Directorate recognized the need to encourage timely reporting of illicit foreign attempts to collect technology or information from cleared contractors. The CI Directorate continued to refine its mission and strategy to identify potentially unlawful penetrators of the cleared industrial base.

Over the course of the year, CI and industrial security personnel worked together to increase CI awareness in industry and to encourage suspicious contact reporting. Each report the agency receives from industry makes a difference. In FY09, federal investigative or intelligence agencies opened 45 investigations or operations based on industry reporting to DSS; in FY10, reports to DSS led to over 200 opened cases.

The case studies below highlight three FY10 threats to the cleared contractor base, and illustrate how DSS collected the threat information and turned it over to law enforcement agencies in record time.

Historically, this process took anywhere from six to twelve months; but as the cases show, DSS has improved its ability to identify, collect, analyze, and disseminate actionable information to other government agencies while increasing analytic proficiency and reducing case backlogs.

Case Study #1:

A cleared contractor received an unsolicited email request from a foreign entity requesting a quote for several export-controlled armaments for an unnamed Middle Eastern client. Because the request was unsolicited and was not received through foreign military sales channels, the cleared contractor reported the incident to the local DSS office. Less than two months later, a U.S. government agency was able to open an investigation based on the information DSS provided.

DSS analysis revealed prior industry reporting concerning the requestor and connected the subject to another suspicious collection attempt under a fake name or alias. Further analysis discovered a known terrorist had previously used that name in email traffic.

Case Study #2:

A foreign entity phoned a cleared contractor attempting to purchase export-controlled aeronautics technology. The individual claimed to be calling on behalf of an unidentified associate seeking the price and delivery information for several aeronautic systems. The cleared contractor considered the incident suspicious given the contact was unsolicited and the requestor withheld the end-user information. The cleared contractor reported the request to the local DSS office and in less than three months, a U.S. government agency opened an investigation based on the information DSS provided.

DSS analysis of the case revealed that the requestor's official business address, residences, and business partners were inconsistent with the information provided with the initial request. Based on these findings, DSS CI determined that the request was likely a third party technology transfer attempt.

Case Study #3:

A foreign person, claiming to be a professor at an East Asian university, requested several export-controlled software systems through a cleared company's public website.

The cleared company reported the incident to the local DSS office and a U.S. government

agency opened an investigation less than three months after the incident occurred. DSS analysis of the case led to the discovery of several relevant published papers regarding aeronautic systems and their military applications.

Research into the foreign university confirmed its involvement in military research and development for an East Asian government. Further analysis connected the foreign university to illicit purchase requests for sensitive U.S. technology and attempts to obtain research positions within several U.S cleared facilities.

DISCO Cases of Interest

The following are unique or unusual cases DISCO reviewed in the past year:

Case Study #1:

DISCO initiated and received results of a periodic reinvestigation. The adjudicator found a cause for concern and asked DSS counterintelligence (CI) personnel to review the incident. DSS CI in turn coordinated with a law enforcement agency which had additional information on the individual.

The individual's clearance eligibility was suspended and the facility was advised of the interim suspension of the eligibility and the need for the individual to be denied access to classified information. Due to privacy issues, the company was not privy to details of the incident.

Case Study #2:

A husband and wife were the key management personnel of a cleared company. A former government employee hired by a cleared company bribed other government officials with gifts to obtain work for the company.

The individuals' clearances were suspended until the company's facility clearance was terminated. In this case, DISCO learned of the situation from third-party sources which identified the company, the individuals, and the government customer.

Case Study #3:

DISCO recommended suspending an individual's interim clearance eligibility based on information that surfaced during the course of a personnel security investigation. The case involved a native born U.S. citizen who exhibited a pattern of questionable behavior. The citizen visited a foreign country on multiple occasions and initiated contact with foreign nationals including unauthorized association with suspected or known agents of a foreign intelligence service that created a potential conflict of interest between the interests of a foreign organization and the United States.

The adjudicator was unable to view the security concerns as having been mitigated based on what was known at the time. Once the personnel security investigation is complete, a decision on the final clearance eligibility will be made.

DSS Operations Analysis Group fosters collaboration and sharing of information

To improve the security of classified U.S. technologies and information under the purview of the National Industrial Security Program (NISP), DSS must ensure that information is shared across the agency. The DSS Operations Analysis Group, established within the CI Directorate, was created to maximize collaboration across the agency, identify gaps in information, and implement solutions

using an approach that fosters interdependent processes between all DSS elements.

During daily, on-site operations meetings, subject matter experts from Industrial Security Field Operations (IO), Industrial Policy and Programs (IP), Counterintelligence (CI) and the Defense Industrial Security Clearance Office (DISCO), discuss unique and complex

security or intelligence issues that impact on DSS operations and policy.

The discussions are designed to reduce the risks posed by foreign directed collection or internal threats to technologies, information, and personnel. By tapping subject matter experts, DSS ensures that each expert brings a unique perspective and a deep understanding of the issues within his or her area of expertise.

To date, three facility clearances have been terminated and 18 personnel security clearance eligibilities have been suspended based on Operations Analysis Group review and recommended action. The following case studies are four examples of how the group has added value by taking seemingly unrelated pieces of information and connected them to form a comprehensive look at a problem.

Case Study #1: No Cleared Key Management Personnel

On June 1, 2010, a cleared facility formally removed its Director from his position amid allegations of financial mismanagement. On June 30, 2010, the facility security officer (FSO) of the facility notified DSS that he was resigning that same day from the facility. As a result, there would not be any cleared key management personnel (KMPs) at the facility (required by paragraph 2-104 of the National Industrial

Security Program Operating Manual (NISPOM)).

On July 1, 2010, DSS personnel met with the new senior management official (who was also serving as the new FSO) to advise and assist with the protection of sensitive DoD information. During this meeting, the new senior management official provided DSS with three suspicious documents linked to the former senior management official.

On July 19, 2010, the DSS Operations Analysis Group received the suspicious contact reports that were submitted in response to the suspicious documents. In less than two weeks, DSS personnel addressed the suspicious documents and counterintelligence concerns linked to the former senior management official and coordinated with both the Industrial Security Field Office to terminate the facility clearance and with the Defense Industrial Security Clearance Office to also terminate appropriate personnel clearances.

This case depicts how DSS connected the dots beginning with a facility request for an "advise and assist" visit and ended with an investigation by another government agency into the former senior management official.

Case Study #2: Jumping Companies

In September 2008, a cleared facility terminated

a Subject's employment based on several security violations that occurred between July and September 2008. In October 2008, this facility entered an incident report and noted the Subject's termination in the Joint Personnel Adjudication System (JPAS). The entries about the subject in JPAS effectively prevented a second cleared facility from reinstating the Subject's access to classified information without an additional background investigation.

In May 2009, a third cleared facility hired the subject. A personnel security investigation was initiated as part of the Subject's employment, during which it was discovered he was collecting proprietary and sensitive information on the company's projects. In February 2010, this third cleared facility terminated the Subject's employment.

In July 2010, the Subject began working for a fourth cleared facility. DSS reinstated the Subject's clearance in error. When the individual received word of his reinstated clearance, he contacted his immediate past employer inquiring about reemployment, as he now had a clearance. This facility contacted DSS, concerned that the individual had received a clearance.

The Operations Analysis Group discovered that the individual's clearance had been reissued in error. DISCO corrected the Subject's JPAS entry in August 2010 to

reflect that he was ineligible for access to classified information until the security issues related to his conduct were resolved. The other government agency's investigation into the individual's activities is continuing.

This case depicts how a Subject tried to move from one cleared company to another to gain a Secret clearance, even though he committed multiple security violations.

Case Study #3: CEO Investigated

In 985, a federal law enforcement agency arrested the Chief Executive Officer (CEO) of a company. The CEO was subsequently convicted of illegally selling electronic eavesdropping equipment.

In the late 1990s, the CEO and his company were both subjects of an industrial espionage investigation. The law enforcement agency involved in that investigation informed DSS that there was a new open investigation concerning the CEO related to terrorism financing allegations.

The DSS Operations Analysis Group provided the Defense Industrial Security Clearance Office (DISCO) with the information and DISCO suspended the CEO's personnel security clearance eligibility.

The suspension of the individual's clearance eligibility meant there were no cleared key management personnel (KMP) at the company.

Without cleared KMP, the facility is ineligible for a facility clearance and the facility's clearance was therefore terminated by DSS at the request of the facility's new CEO.

This case depicts cross-agency coordination involving a cleared contractor and facility with ties to industrial espionage and a likely foreign terrorist organization.

Case Study #4: Outside Referral

During a 2007 interview for employment with a government agency (Agency 1), the Subject admitted to removing classified information from his office while he was interning at another government organization in 2004 (Agency 2).

The Subject, who was asked to reproduce classified documents while working at Agency 2, even though he did not have the necessary clearance, stated he took the classified information home as a souvenir.

Agency 1 advised the Subject to return the classified information and did not hire him. The Subject returned most of the classified information; however, 10 documents are still unaccounted for.

Subsequently, Agency 1's Office of Security submitted this information as a hotline tip to a DoD criminal investigative agency in June 2010. While validating the information, that agency discovered that the Subject was cleared and was working for a contractor cleared under the NISP. DSS received the information in June 2010.

The DSS Operations Analysis Group referred this case to several law enforcement agencies in July 2010. Based on the information and the severity of the mishandling of classified information while he worked for Agency 2, DSS suspended the Subject's clearance.

The investigation is continuing, and DSS is supporting the law enforcement investigations with relevant information. This case depicts cross-agency coordination, leading to an investigation/operation by other Government agencies.

DSS Priorities & Future

For the coming year, DSS will continue to enhance and expand its oversight of the National Industrial Security Program and reinvigorate the Security Education, Training and Awareness Program. Our priorities are the following:

- Renew and strengthen the partnership between Government and Industry Stakeholders for the betterment of national security in this evolving security environment

- Continue to provide support to the cleared industrial base to ensure it is effective in detecting and mitigating threats

- Develop and implement a coordinated cybersecurity strategy across DSS and support industry in its efforts to deter cyberattacks

- Continue timely resolution of FOCI cases and provide enhanced FOCI oversight and analysis

- Establish an Insider Threat Program within DSS

- Complete BRAC-mandated moves to Marine Corps Base Quantico, Va., and Fort George G. Meade, Md., with no degradation of service

66 *In short, our intelligence community needs to work as one integrated team that produces quality, timely, and accurate intelligence. And ... this is a tough task.* 99

Barack H. Obama
President of the United States

- Continue development and implementation of the DoD Security Professional Education Development (SPēD) Certification Program

- Expand tailored inspection program to freight forwarders and Arms, Ammunition, & Explosives (AA&E) facilities

- Develop a procedure to standardize the security rating process nationwide in order to reduce subjectivity and increase consistency

- Reestablish an overseas industrial security presence

- Continue integration of counterintelligence into all aspects of DSS operations

www.ingramcontent.com/pod-product-compliance
Lightning Source LLC
Chambersburg PA
CBHW080737290526
45790CB00008B/3225